Bones, Brains and DNA
The Human Genome and Human Evolution

by Ian Tattersall & Rob DeSalle

ILLUSTRATED BY PATRICIA J. WYNNE

Based on the New Hall of Human Origins at the **American Museum of Natural History**

BUNKER HILL PUBLISHING

No. Those ideas called theories that have been tested and aren't rejected are the ones that scientists use to explain nature.

I get it. A theory that has been tested over and over again and not rejected can be pretty close to the truth.

That's it!

Science is ...

A lot of people don't know it, but there are over 300 scientists working behind the scenes in the buildings of the American Museum of Natural History. These scientists work on discovering the origins of natural things all the way from rocks to stars (the geologists and astrophysicists) and from bacteria to dinosaurs (the **zoologists** and **paleontologists**). At the museum, human beings have their own scientists called **anthropologists.** The tools and objects that scientists use to understand the natural world range from microscopes to telescopes, from rulers to computers, and, most important for human origins, from **genomes** to bones.

The job of a scientist is very different from any other. Science is about trying to explain things as best we can, since there is no way to know all the true answers to questions about nature. This is especially the case when we talk about the origins of humans. Scientists systematically test ideas over and over again, rejecting those ideas that are wrong.
The positive result of these many tests becomes a **theory**. Many theories are almost certainly facts, but scientists most often do not call them facts. The ideas contained in theories can be used in medicine, engineering, architecture, agriculture, industry, and a wide array of things that can be very useful to humans and their health and well-being.

SEED BEAK

WOODPECKER BEAK

The American Museum of Natural History is one of the world's largest storage closets for nature. Over 31 million specimens are stored within the museum's walls. There are also huge laboratories where scientists prepare bones, isolate DNA, and study geological and paleontological specimens.

There are a lot of anthropology halls in the museum ...

... because there are so many kinds of anthropology.

Anthropology is ...

Most people aren't sure exactly what **anthropologists** do, and that's because there are so many different kinds of anthropologists. Anthropology is the scientific quest to understand more about people. But people have lots of different aspects to them. This is why so many different areas of science have become involved in this quest. Broadly speaking, though, anthropologists come in three kinds:

There are the **cultural anthropologists**, who observe how people behave and how the societies in which they live function. Societies are incredibly diverse and live in an amazing variety of climates and habitats, and as a result they have developed a huge number of ways of viewing and dealing with each other and with the **environments** they live in.

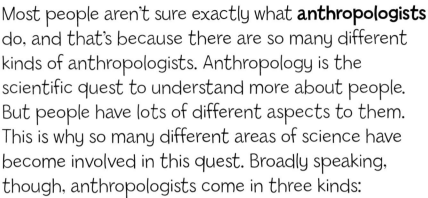

Here's the Hall of African Peoples. It shows how many different African societies lived and what they made.

4

On to the Hall of Mexico and Central America. Here are things about the amazing civilizations that flourished south of the United States before Europeans came.

Wow! The museum is packed with fabulous objects showing what people can achieve with their hands and minds.

Then there are the **archaeologists**, who look at the record of their lives that earlier societies and generations have left behind them. In this way they reconstruct the past of the human species from times before there were any books or other written evidence.

And finally there are the **biological anthropologists**. Some of these study how people vary across the world today and how they cope with different environmental issues. Others, known as paleoanthropologists, look at the fossilized bones of human ancestors and extinct relatives to learn how human beings became the creatures they are.

This is only the tip of the iceberg. Come this way ...

Paleontology is ...

Everybody knows that paleontologists study **fossils**, but few people are aware how many kinds of paleontologists there are. Some paleontologists study how the bones of dead animals get turned to stone after they die, and then become preserved in accumulating piles of rock. Others put those bones together and try to figure out how those animals lived and moved when they were alive. Still others try to understand how different fossil animals were related to each other, and to animals that are alive today. Or they may be involved in figuring out how old the fossils are, or what kind of **environments** they lived in, and on and on ...

Dinosaurs!
They ruled the Earth between about 350 and 65 million years ago. Many were huge. Some were tiny. And some had feathers, which show they were related to birds.

Then, 65 million years ago there was a mass extinction. Some sudden event, maybe an asteroid crashing into the Earth, killed the dinosaurs and lots of other creatures.

The fossils themselves can be very old. The oldest fossils we know of are microscopic creatures that are almost 4 billion years old. The oldest animals with backbones go back well over 500 million years. Those animals lived in the sea; the first land-living animals first ventured ashore about 370 million years ago. Life has been diverse almost from the beginning. It seems that Nature is constantly experimenting with new ways for living things to take advantage of the environments around them.

The animals in here look rather different. Did they come next?

Some tiny nocturnal creatures called mammals took over the planet. Their descendants diversified and eventually led to us mice ... and people.

T rex actual size tooth
early mammal

7

Evolution is ...

Charles Darwin was led to the idea of evolution 150 years ago when he wondered why all of the living things in the world seemed to belong to groups that in turn belonged to larger groups. He saw, for example, that of all the many animals out there, humans most closely resembled the **great apes**, and that as a group, the two both most closely resembled the **monkeys**. All together, they seemed to belong to a great group that included all of the furry mammals, among them mice. How was this pattern of **resemblance** achieved? Darwin thought that it must be due to common ancestry: that humans and apes shared a quite **recent common ancestor**, that humans plus apes shared a rather more ancient ancestor with the monkeys, and so forth. And today this remains the best—indeed the only—scientific explanation for what Darwin saw.

Charles Darwin

Gosh, there's an awful lot you need to know about genes!

But once you know it, there's a lot genes can tell us about EVOLUTION.

Right! What's evolution about? Has everything evolved?

Everything has evolved. You and me - and people, too. In fact, once, we all had the same ancestor.

lemur

tree shrew

human

ape

monkey

mouse

8

This meant, of course, that living forms must change with time, so Darwin needed to explain how this might happen. Knowing that all individuals vary a bit in their **inherited characteristics** (as we now realize, through random changes in **genes** called mutations), Darwin proposed that such change occurs through "**natural selection**." Individuals with favorable "**adaptations**" leave more offspring. In this way the population changes as good new variations become steadily more common. Nowadays it is clear that several different factors may help to explain the patterns of change and resemblance that we see, but most everyone is happy to accept Darwin's definition of evolution as "**descent with modification**."

Darwin sketched a tree of life

This page fro Darwin's notebook was the very first "family tree" to represent the relationships among different species.

That's wild, isn't it! Millions and millions of years ago, right around the time when the dinosaurs died out, all of us mammals had a common ancestor.

And this is what it may have looked like. Tiny and furry, more like an insectivore or a bat than like us mice. And it probably was active at night.

Come on. Let's see what's next

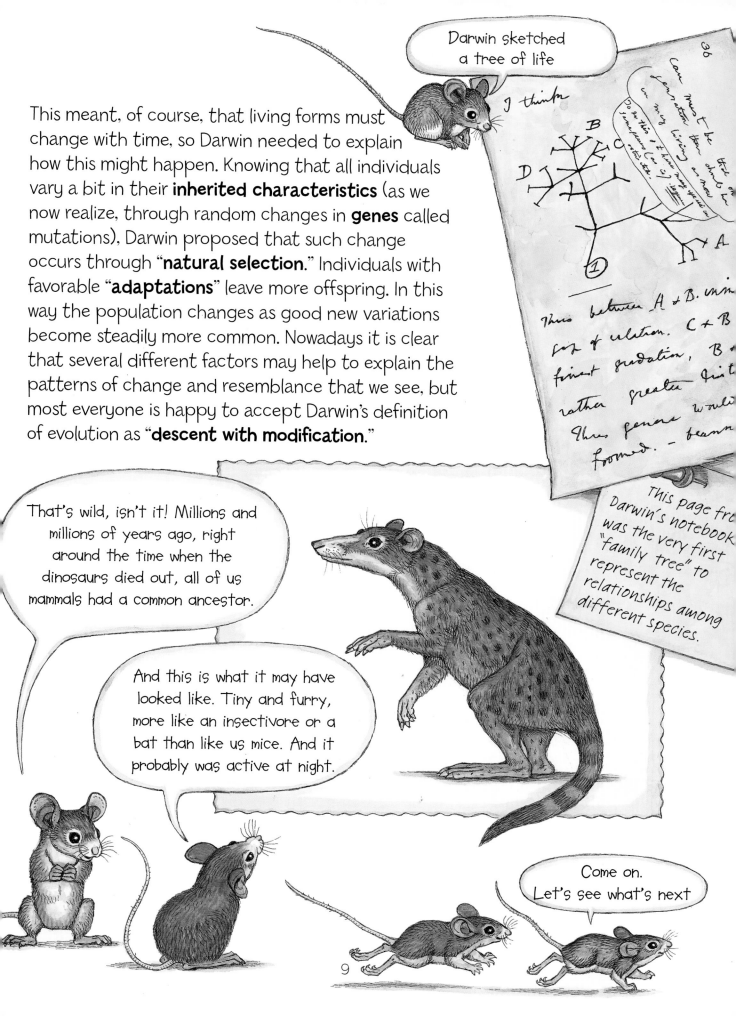

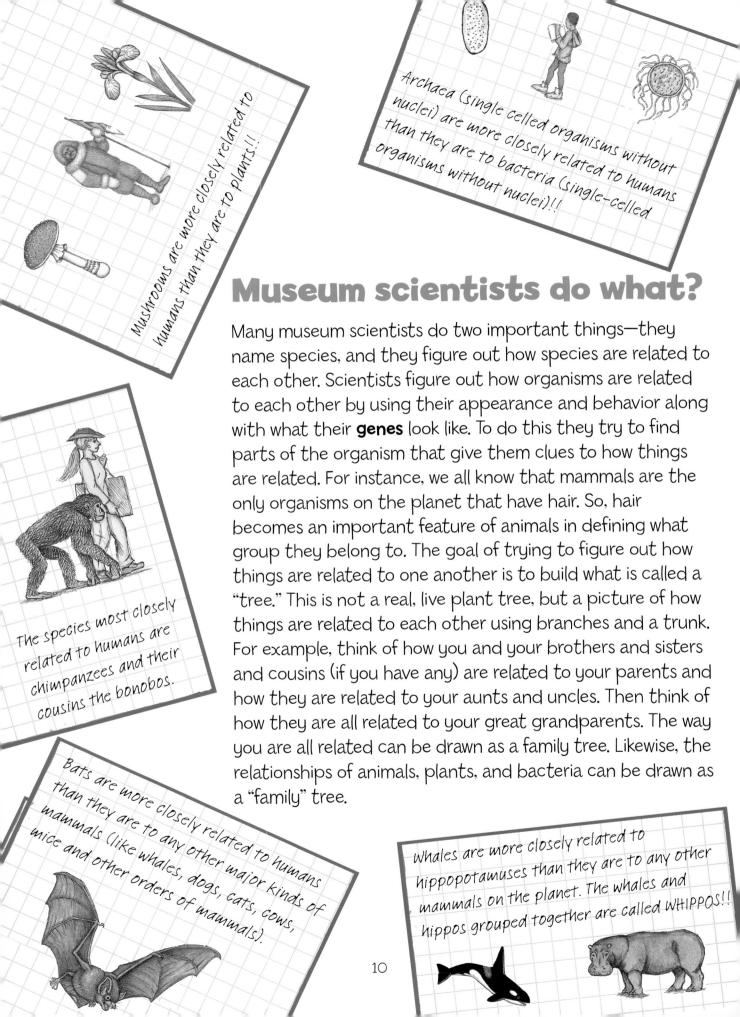

Mushrooms are more closely related to humans than they are to plants!!

Archaea (single celled organisms without nuclei) are more closely related to humans than they are to bacteria (single-celled organisms without nuclei)!!

Museum scientists do what?

Many museum scientists do two important things—they name species, and they figure out how species are related to each other. Scientists figure out how organisms are related to each other by using their appearance and behavior along with what their **genes** look like. To do this they try to find parts of the organism that give them clues to how things are related. For instance, we all know that mammals are the only organisms on the planet that have hair. So, hair becomes an important feature of animals in defining what group they belong to. The goal of trying to figure out how things are related to one another is to build what is called a "tree." This is not a real, live plant tree, but a picture of how things are related to each other using branches and a trunk. For example, think of how you and your brothers and sisters and cousins (if you have any) are related to your parents and how they are related to your aunts and uncles. Then think of how they are all related to your great grandparents. The way you are all related can be drawn as a family tree. Likewise, the relationships of animals, plants, and bacteria can be drawn as a "family" tree.

The species most closely related to humans are chimpanzees and their cousins the bonobos.

Bats are more closely related to humans than they are to any other major kinds of mammals (like whales, dogs, cats, cows, mice and other orders of mammals).

Whales are more closely related to hippopotamuses than they are to any other mammals on the planet. The whales and hippos grouped together are called WHIPPOS!!

Tree of life

This tree will show the major branches of life and indicate that all life on earth comes from a common ancestor.

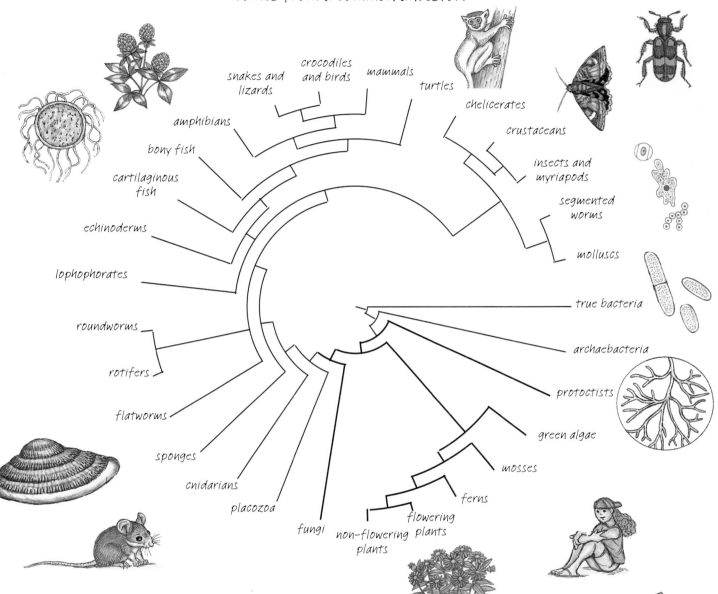

How to read a tree

The creatures (we are going to call plants creatures, too) at the tips of the tree are usually living creatures. If you can trace two creatures back to a trunk, and no other creatures are traced back to that trunk, then the two are each other's closest relative, or the two have an ancestor in common. The process is repeated over and again all over the tree.

For naming organisms we still use the system of two-part names established by Carl Linnaeus 250 years ago. The first name gives the genus, the second gives the species.

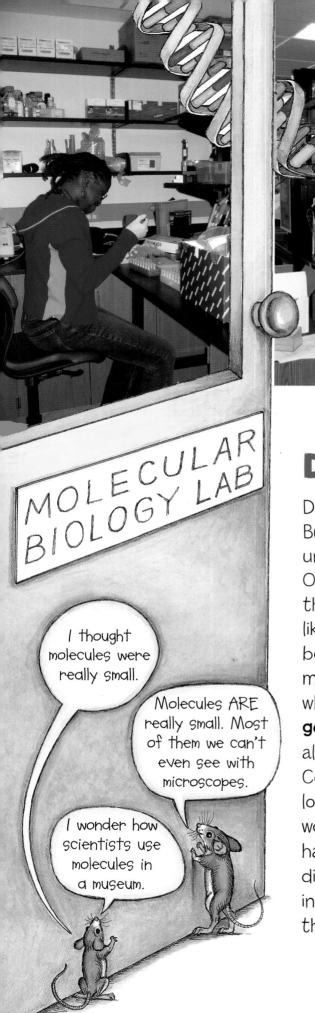

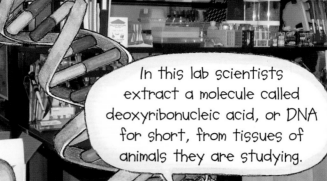

In this lab scientists extract a molecule called deoxyribonucleic acid, or DNA for short, from tissues of animals they are studying.

Right! They use DNA to figure out the relationships of organisms.

I thought molecules were really small.

Molecules ARE really small. Most of them we can't even see with microscopes.

I wonder how scientists use molecules in a museum.

MOLECULAR BIOLOGY LAB

DNA is ...

Deoxyribonucleic Acid—it's a long term, right? But it's actually a pretty simple thing to understand. We call this stuff DNA for short. One way to look at what DNA is and does is to think of it as writing in a book, and DNA is kind of like the alphabet that makes up the words in the book. Then, think of the book as the **cells** that make up our bodies—us. The words tell our cells what to do. The "words" made up of DNA are called **genes**. Does DNA have 26 letters like our English alphabet? NO! DNA only has four letters. Consequently, with only four letters, the DNA words look nothing like our English words or any **language's** words for that matter. The four letters scientists have chosen to use are GATC, and they represent different small **molecules** that are strung together in these "gene sentences." What kind of words are they? Well, instead of words like CAT and DOG,

YOU can make DNA

DNA IN A TUBE

1 Pour a package of baker's yeast from your refrigerator into half a glass of water. ¹/₂ glass of water

2 Sprinkle a pinch of salt into the yeast-water solution. Mix it well. pinch of salt

3 Add 10 drops of liquid dishwashing soap into the solution. 10 drops, liquid dishwasher soap

the combination of letters makes words that are instructions for your cells to make molecules called proteins that make your cells work.

Just as words have to be spelled correctly and in the right order to understand language, the words in the DNA "Book" must be spelled correctly and in the right order for the cell to make the right proteins. A sentence might read something like:

THE CAT SAT ON THE TREE, but if a change occurs in one letter it might say: THE BAT SAT ON THE TREE, and the meaning of the sentence would change.

Just as these small changes change the meaning of the sentence, so it is with genes. If the spelling or the order of the DNA molecules is changed the entire gene might change what it does. These changes are called "mutations," and they are the stuff that evolution is made of.

Now that you know about what DNA is, you can ask: Where is it, and it what does it look like? Because there are many different ways to look at DNA, this is a hard question to answer. For now, let's just answer it by saying what it looks like in two different ways. At one extreme the GATCs are strung together like beads on a string and make a **double helix**. On the other extreme, DNA looks like phlegm when a bunch of it is placed in a tube (see kitchen experiment).

4 rubbing alcohol, water

Here's the part your parents can do. Have them slowly pour rubbing alcohol down the side of the glass until it is full.

Let the mixture sit for a few minutes. You will see some white stuff drift up into the alcohol layer. The white stuff is yeast DNA!

Speech bubble: This idea of the museum using DNA boggles the mind. Where does DNA come from?

ORGANISM

ORGAN

DNA comes from where?

Let's go on a journey into your eye, where every time we get closer, we also magnify what we see. As you get closer and closer to the eye you begin to see different **tissues**. And as you get closer to the tissues, you start to see **cells**. Part of the eye is made up of cells called rods and **cones**, named so because they look like rods and cones. As you get closer to a cone cell, you start to make out the various parts of the cell. You can see **mitochondria**, small blobs where energy is made. You can also see what looks like mazes in the body of the cell. These are called endoplasmic reticulum, where the cell manufactures products that keep it alive. But the most spectacular thing you can see about a cell is that it looks as if there is another cell or body within it. This large cell-like thing is called a **nucleus**. When we zoom in on the nucleus, we start to see big "stringy" things that look like bundles of wire. These bundles are

Speech bubble: Remember that story about the mouse that ate the cheese, and the cat that ate the mouse and the dog that ate the cat ...

Speech bubble: Enough already!! What does that have to do with DNA?

CELL (CONE)

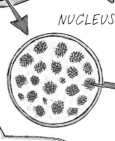

NUCLEUS

ROD
CONE

Speech bubble: Understanding where DNA comes from is kinda like that story. DNA comes first, and it is part of a gene. The gene is part of a chromosome and a chromosome is part of a nucleus, a nucleus is part of a cell, cells are parts of tissues like muscles, and tissues are what we are made of.

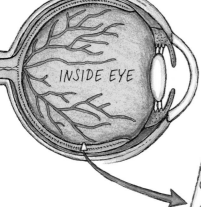

INSIDE EYE

TISSUE
(RETINA)

called **chromosomes**. In the cone cell we have zoomed in on, there are 46 of these chromosomes.

We pick one chromosome to zoom in on even further, and as we start to see it unravel like a ball of string, we realize that the chromosome is actually a long, long string of something. Zooming in even further, we notice even smaller stretches on the chromosome that are called **genes**. We zoom on by the genes, and as we begin to magnify more, we start to see that the genes are actually made of two strings wound around each other like a spiral staircase. The last thing we see as we reach the DNA are the chemical arrangements of the atoms that make up the four DNA letters–G, A, T, and C.

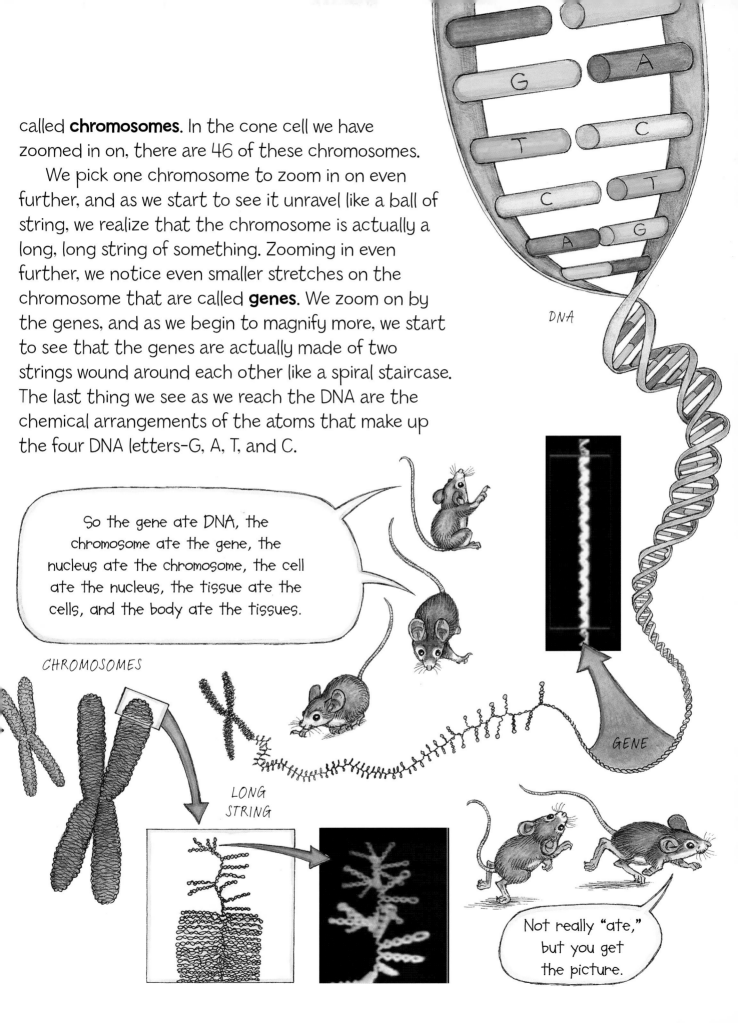

DNA

So the gene ate DNA, the chromosome ate the gene, the nucleus ate the chromosome, the cell ate the nucleus, the tissue ate the cells, and the body ate the tissues.

CHROMOSOMES

LONG STRING

GENE

Not really "ate," but you get the picture.

Sequencing is ...

Remember that DNA is made up of many small **molecules** connected to one another that have the names GATC. Several chemical steps are done to each gene in order to sequence it. The **DNA sequence** of a complete set of **chromosomes** of an organism is called a **genome**. The "robots" and automated sequencer are machines that actually read the "sequence" of GATCs from the **gene**. When all of the genes and the DNA in between the genes is known, the gene sequences can be put together like a puzzle, and Voila! An entire genome of a creature is obtained. The entire genomes of about 500 organisms have been sequenced in the last ten years.

DNA is so small that scientists need a machine called an automated DNA sequencer to look at it.

Automated? Does that mean it's like a robot?

Yup. There is so much DNA to sequence for organisms like humans, robots are needed to do almost everything.

Robots that walk around and talk?

Ahem ... These robots are really machines and computers that repeat the motions involved in the sequencing process over and over again.

The first genome sequenced of an organism was from a bacterium called *Haemophilus influenza* or H flu for short. H flu's genome is about 2 million GATCs long. The human genome has been sequenced and it is about 3 billion GATCs long. Two million GATCs one after another, in the same size print as on this page, would stretch about 3 miles. Three billion GATCs in the same size print as on this page would stretch all the way across the United States from New York City to Los Angeles and beyond.

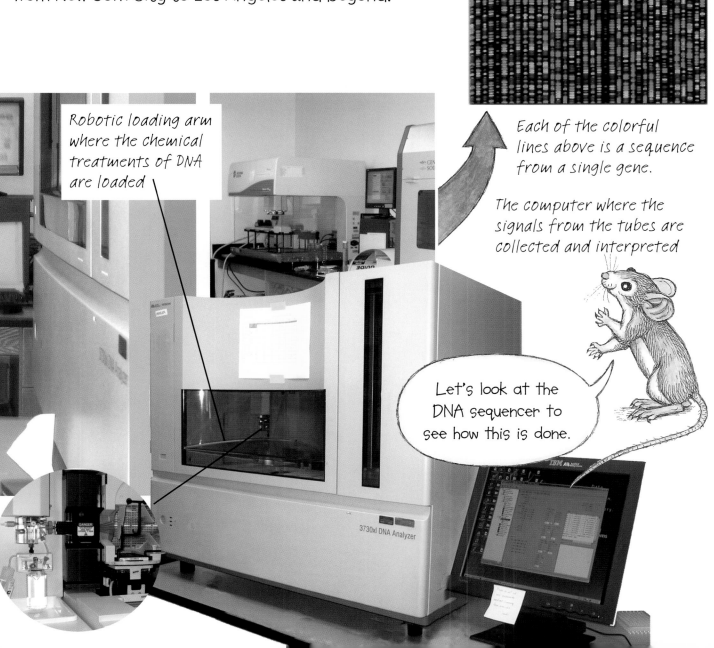

The final product is a colorful print-out showing how the GATC letters are arranged in a gene.

Robotic loading arm where the chemical treatments of DNA are loaded

Each of the colorful lines above is a sequence from a single gene.

The computer where the signals from the tubes are collected and interpreted

Let's look at the DNA sequencer to see how this is done.

3730xl DNA Analyzer

What's in a Genome?

Our genomes have 22 pairs of a certain kind of **chromosome** called **AUTOSOMES** and one pair of chromosomes called **SEX CHROMOSOMES**, because this last pair is involved in determining whether a person will be a girl or a boy. Chromosomes are nothing more than bundles of **genes**. Note how they are numbered. They are numbered from the largest, which is called chromosome 1, to the smallest, called chromosome 22. The stripes on the chromosomes in the figure represent places on the chromosome where DNA condenses and makes tight blocks of DNA. The biggest chromosome is over 200,000,000 GATCs long, and the shortest is a little over 50,000,000. The genes on the chromosomes are lined up along the length of each chromosome. Y chromosomes are found only in males. The Y chromosome has very few genes on it. There are only about 70 to 300 genes on this small chromosome. Females have two X chromosomes and males have only one. The X chromosome has between 2,100 and 2,600 genes on it. Knowing the sequences of all of the genes on the 22 autosomes and 1 pair of sex chromosomes allows scientists to examine the **hereditary** basis of disease, behavior, and human anatomy and development. **DNA sequences** also can be used to tell us how humans evolved.

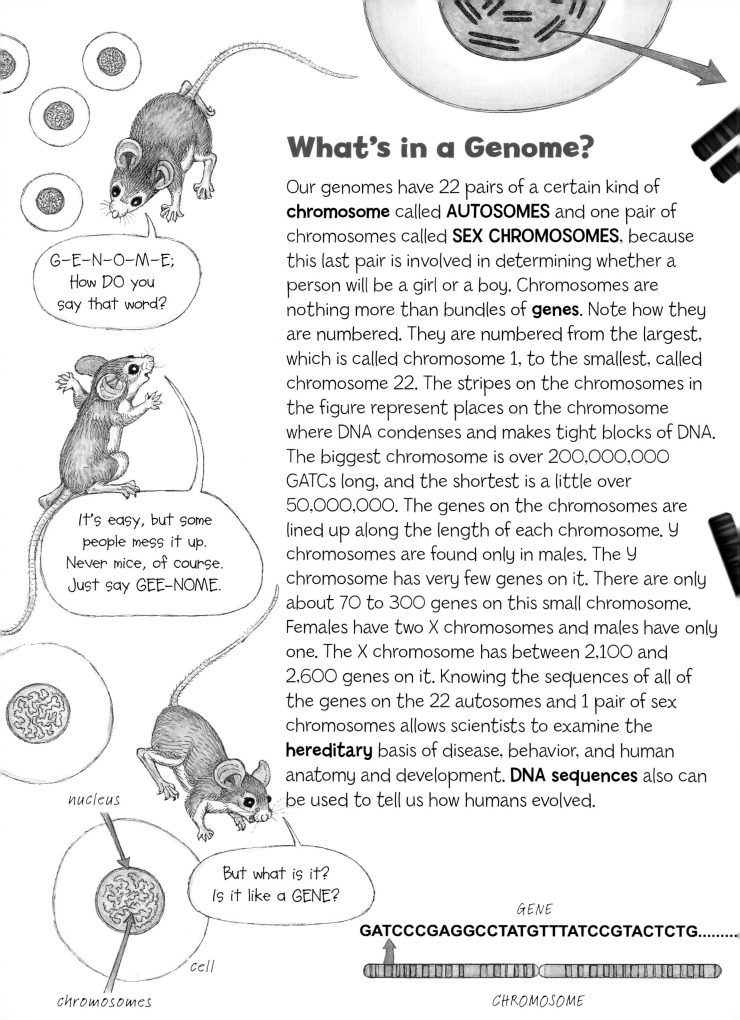

G-E-N-O-M-E; How DO you say that word?

It's easy, but some people mess it up. Never mice, of course. Just say GEE-NOME.

But what is it? Is it like a GENE?

nucleus

cell

chromosomes

GENE

GATCCCGAGGCCTATGTTTATCCGTACTCTG.........

CHROMOSOME

Your genome is the collection of all of the genes in your cells. AND all of the other DNA that helps keep track of your DNA as cells divide. Remember there are 3 billion GATCs in your genome.

We mice have about 3 billion GATCs in our genome.

And each of your cells has the same number of genes, and, in fact, they are the same genes. We mice and humans, as well as most other furry mammals, have about 30,000 genes.

HUMAN CHROMOSOMES

That's a lot. How do our cells keep track of that much information? One way is to organize the 30,000 genes and 3 billion GATCs into small bundles of DNA called chromosomes. Our friends the humans have 23 pairs of these chromosomes.

GEE! ... (NOME)

Ouch! Bad joke!

19

Can you guess what those numbers mean?

The first number represents the amount of the human genome that is similar to the chimpanzee genome.

Scientists have sequenced the genomes of many other living things including ours ... and rats.

DNA in a small tube

Chimps look really similar to humans. Mice and rats must be much less similar to humans, right?

Wrong. We have about 85 to 90% the same genes as humans.

Okay, I can guess what 99.9% means. It's the amount of the genome similar between individual humans.

98.7 and 99.9% mean ...

How can chimpanzees, who look and act so different from us, have so much of their **genome similar** to ours? The answer lies in WHERE that 1.3% difference is. Most scientists suggest that the differences are in regions of **genes** that control how they are expressed. Because these regions control **gene expression**, they can turn genes on and off and regulate the amount of products made from the genes, much as a faucet can regulate the amount of water going into your bathtub. Because gene products are critical to how different structures in the body are made, different regulation of gene products in chimpanzees can produce the differences we see between humans and chimpanzees.

We humans are a pretty diverse group of organisms, yet there is only a 0.1% gene difference between any two randomly chosen humans (unless they are related). Or is this really a small difference? If there are 3 billion GATC's in our genome, 0.1% would be 3 million GATC's that are different between you and any randomly chosen individual, no matter what they look like. Why? Because for long periods of time we have mated and had children with each other, regardless of what we look like.

You got it!

Chimpanzees have 23 pairs of **autosomes** and 1 pair of **sex chromosomes**. Almost all of the **chromosomes** in chimpanzees are also found in humans, except that chromosome 2 is missing in chimps, and chromosomes 12 and 13 of the chimpanzee are missing in humans. How did chimpanzees get the extra chromosome, or how did humans lose a chromosome? The answer is like putting a puzzle together. In the figure, the middle, long chromosome is human chromosome 2. The chromosome to the right is chimpanzee chromosome 12 and the chromosome to the left is chimpanzee chromosome 13. The puzzle pieces fit by looking at the bands on the chromosomes and matching the patterns from human to chimpanzee. That was easy! Now look at the mouse human puzzle. In this case only the pink chromosome (the X) is found in both mice and humans. The rest are a mess and prettier to look at than to decipher.

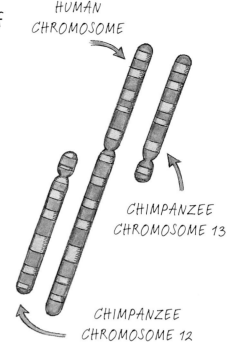

HUMAN CHROMOSOME

CHIMPANZEE CHROMOSOME 13

CHIMPANZEE CHROMOSOME 12

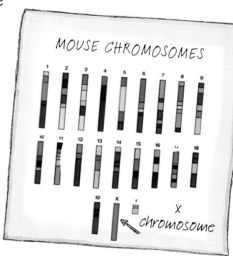

MOUSE CHROMOSOMES

X chromosome

Here are human chromosomes. How many do they have?

Wow! Our chromosomes are really jumbled up!

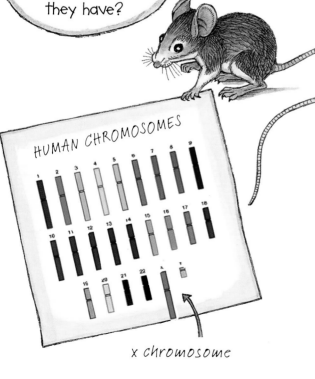

HUMAN CHROMOSOMES

x chromosome

To get this figure, the human chromosomes are cut into about 100 or so pieces. Then the human chromosome pieces are matched to their place in the mouse chromosomes and pasted down in that position until all 100 pieces are pasted into the puzzle.

Humans have 30,000 genes. Does that mean they have more genes than anything else on Earth? Mice are interesting animals. I think we should have more genes.

FRUIT FLY

YEAST

36%

23%

All organisms share some genes in common, and the more genes they have in common the more they tend to resemble each other.

Mice DO have as many genes as humans do. We have lots more of some kinds of genes.

We gotta have more than humans.

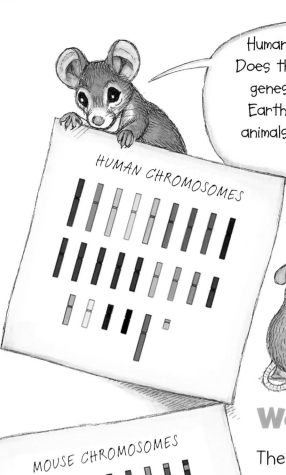

HUMAN CHROMOSOMES

MOUSE CHROMOSOMES

CHIMPANZEE CHROMOSOMES

We are all alike

There are many ways to look at how **similar genes** and **genomes** are. The first way is to examine the order of the DNA letters in the genes. We have already talked about mutations and how they change proteins, but these mutations can be used to understand how creatures are related to each other, too. Another way of looking at how organisms are similar to each other is by examining their **chromosomes**. Remember that when chimp and human chromosomes are compared, the big chromosome 2 in humans is discovered to be chromosome 12 and 13 from the chimpanzee. A different picture emerges if you look at the mouse and human chromosomes. In this case, the chromosome puzzle can be put together, but it is much more jumbled than the chimpanzee picture. A final thing that we can look at to say how similar we are genetically to other organisms is to count how many genes a creature has and how many of these genes humans have in common with that creature. For

Well ... not for the brain. People have more of those, but mice have hundreds more genes for smell.

CHIMPANZEE

THALE CRESS

15% →

99%

E COLI

7%

So, mice and humans have lots of kinds of different kinds of genes.

Says here about 90-95% of the genes in our mouse genome are the same kinds of genes as humans.

ZEBRA FISH

23%

85%

95% MOUSE

ROUND WORM

Wow! I wonder how come we look so different.

instance, we saw in the last chapter that chimpanzees have about the same number of genes, and of those genes, 98.7% are same kinds of genes that humans have. This number drops to 90-95% for mice. Just to give you an idea of how related we are to all creatures on the planet, think of this— humans have 30,000 genes, mice have 30,000, flies have 22,000, worms have 19,000, yeast (that stuff that makes bread) has 6,000 genes, some plants have 30,000, and bacteria have between 400 and 12,000 genes. So, there really is no sense to how many genes a creature has and how complex it is. More surprising is that humans and all of these other creatures have many of the same genes. Mice share 95% of our genes, flies share 36%, worms about 21%, yeast 23%, plants about 18% and even bacteria share 7% of their genes with humans. What does this mean? It means that all life on this planet had a common ancestor that existed over 3 billion years ago.

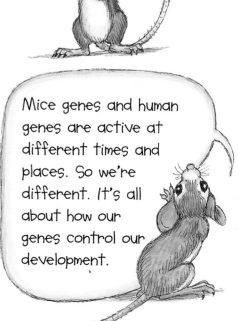

Mice genes and human genes are active at different times and places. So we're different. It's all about how our genes control our development.

Are genes all that is making me what I am?

Our **genomes** have all of the **hereditary** information needed to produce a human. But the final appearance of an organism, whether it be in its body or the way it acts, results from an interaction of the **genes** and the **environment**. We must always remember this when attempting to make sense of traits in humans and other organisms. Many problems in human health that scientists are confronting involve complex traits. For instance, asthma has many genes involved in it. Some of the genes contribute more to whether someone has asthma than others, and, of course, the environment can trigger asthma. Being way overweight is also controlled by many genes, of which a few are really, really important. And again, your environment, in this case your diet, will be a huge factor in whether or not you are overweight. Another factor involved in making us who we are, is how we develop. Recently, scientists have discovered some very interesting genes that control the development

Wow! Lots of genes and DNA are everywhere then. Does that mean we are programmed to be the way we are by our genes?

NO and YES. Our environment has a major effect on how our genes are expressed as traits. Here's the easiest way to look at it. Some traits that are parts of us, like our eyes, our noses, our legs are very much controlled by genes.

Other things like how tall we are and how fast we run have a mixture of environment and genes.

There must be other things that the environment has a huge effect on, like intelligence and whether or not we like to fight?

of organisms. Surprisingly, these genes are found in all kinds of organisms, from sponges to insects to fish to humans. All over the animal world these genes define where our heads are and where our arms are. Other genes refine the development of our body parts. Scientists can look at embryos of developing mice (don't tell our friends roaming through the museum in this book), and ascertain where certain genes are turned on and where they are turned off. Oftentimes, the genes are turned on in very precise ways, and in these cases the genes can be said to be very important for that part of our body.

These are some complex traits . . .
Musical and artistic ability
Asthma
Intelligence
Height
Weight

MOUSE EMBRYO

True, but even for the same trait in two different organisms, the amount of the genes' effects and the environment's effect might differ.

FRUIT FLY

How smart you are might involve more of your genes than for me. I might be as smart as I am because of the environment I have lived in.

Complex!

Exactly. That's what geneticists call these traits – COMPLEX TRAITS.

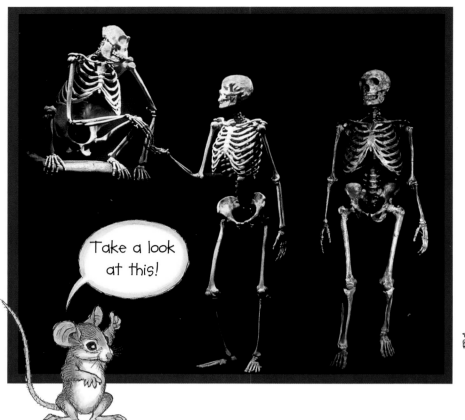

Take a look at this!

Gorilla

Orangutan

Lemur

These are the skeletons of a gorilla, a Neanderthal, and a modern human.

They symbolize what this Hall is all about: that all of us share a common ancestor.

Even though one is on all fours and the other two are standing upright?

Right! Neanderthals and modern humans are very close relatives, and both are upright walkers, while chimps aren't. Hum ... none of them has a tail.

EVOLVING PRIMATES
by
Jay H. Matternes

That's because the most rece ancestor of apes and humans di have a tail, even though it live the trees like other primate

Human Ancestors

The Hall of Human Origins at the American Museum of Natural History contains the story of how human beings evolved to be the creatures we are today. It starts by showing us that human beings are primates: that we belong to the great group that also includes not only the **great apes** (the chimpanzee, gorilla, and orangutan) and the **monkeys**, but also the beautiful **lemurs** of Madagascar and the shy, night-living bushbabies and **lorises** of Africa and Asia. There are more than 200 living species of primates!

The common ancestor of all the primates lived more than 60 million years ago. It lived in the trees and used claws for climbing, unlike primates today. After a while its cat-sized descendants came to look more like the lemurs, with hands that could grasp branches between the thumb and fingers. But even though they had nails and sensitive fingertips, they still explored the world around them mostly with their longish noses.

The ancestor of the monkeys, apes, and people probably lived around 30 million years ago, but the earliest **fossils** we know that might be closely related to the ancestor we share only with the great apes (maybe just with one of them), come from no more than about 11 million years ago. These ancestors still lived in the trees, but they had bigger **brains**, even compared to their rather larger bodies, than any primates that came before them. And they used their eyes much more than their noses.

Gibbon

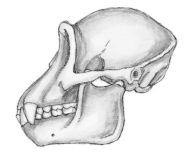

Chimp skull

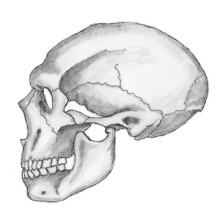

Neanderthal skull

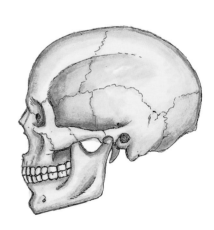

Modern Human skull

No tail? What a shame!

Look at this amazing scene. It's a model of an archaeological site, at La Micoque, in France.

See all those people. They're archaeologists, digging to see what ancient people were doing there 300,000 years ago.

The cave site of Arago in southern France was inhabited by humans 400,000 years ago.

How do we know?

Reconstructing the human past isn't easy. In the Hall of Human Origins we are shown some of the ways in which scientists, working like detectives, put together all kinds of indirect clues left behind by our ancestors to create a rounded picture of their lives. Many different kinds of scientists are involved in this quest. Some of them are **paleontologists** who specialize in the study of human **fossils** and who work with all those kinds of specialists we already met in Chapter 3. But one kind of scientist is unique to the study of the human past.

This is the **archaeologist**. **Archaeology** is the branch of science that studies the traces left behind by early human activities. In early stages these traces are simple, such as **stone tools** or the cut-marks they

Every archaeological site has lots of different specialists working at it. Let's see what they're doing.

Most of the people here are carefully excavating. But others are making maps of what is found where. Others are identifying animal bones, or taking pollen samples, or any number of different things ...

made on ancient animal bones. With time, they became more complex, including such things as campsites with fireplaces and the bones of animals that were cooked and eaten there. But complicated structures such as buildings made out of stone and mud brick did not show up until well after modern people had arrived.

For archaeologists and human paleontologists alike, knowing how old ancient fossils and artifacts are is extremely important. Early **dating methods** only told you what was older or younger than what, but in the last half-century, techniques have been developed that will sometimes give you a date in years. These depend on the "radioactive clock," which "ticks" because unstable forms of atoms change to stable ones at known and steady rates.

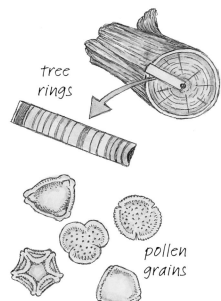

animal bones

tree rings

pollen grains

Stone Tools

In early times most of the objects found by **archaeologists** were stone tools. This is because stone is extremely durable, in contrast to wood and fibers that rot away extremely quickly. Of course, stone tools tell only a tiny part of the story of early human activities, but since they are usually all or most of what we have, archaeologists have had to learn to extract the maximum amount of information from them.

Look at all these stone tools. They don't look like much, do they?

Yes, but they are carefully made to a standard shape.

And the very first tools were simple sharp flakes.

Stone tools showed up for the first time only about 2 ½ million years ago. They are not very impressive, just sharp flakes knocked off one stone by another. But they were revolutionary in the lives of early humans, allowing our small-bodied ancestors to cut pieces off animal carcasses they found, and carry them away to safe places to be eaten. And they were very effective: archaeologists have used replicas of these tools to butcher entire elephants.

They also tell us a lot about the mental abilities of those ancestors. To make even crude stone tools like these, you have to be able to recognize the right kind of rock. And then you have to know how to hit it at exactly the right angle to knock off a sharp flake. No modern ape, even with a lot of coaching, has been able to grasp this idea. What's more, we know that the early tool makers carried lumps of rock around the landscape before making them into tools, so they had some capacity for foresight and planning.

using stone tools

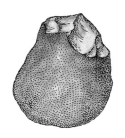

rock *sharp flake*

Archeologists know from cut-marks on bones that they used tools like this to cut up animal carcasses, sometimes of quite big animals.

Animals they'd killed?

Probably not. These early toolmakers were pretty small-bodied and vulnerable away from the trees. But maybe they were good at stealing bits of animals killed by predators like leopards.

Aren't they cute! They are re-creations of the hominids that made the famous footprint trails at Laetoli, in Tanzania, about 3½ million years ago. They are often called "bipedal apes" because they had small brains and very big faces.

See over here? This is much later in time, when people with bodies a lot like those of modern people began to spread across the Old World.

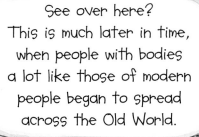

And here's a scene set near Beijing in China, maybe half a million years ago. It shows how vulnerable early hominids were to predatory animals.

stone handaxe

Early Humans

The human story goes back well beyond the first **stone tool** makers, though. At around 7 million years ago the continent of Africa was becoming drier, and more open spaces appeared in the forests. This created opportunities for some of the ape-like primates living in the **forest canopy**. At least for some of the time, they would descend to the ground, where they moved around on their hind limbs, probably because they were already most comfortable holding their bodies upright in the trees.

These were the first **hominids**—members of our own family of primates. They were pretty small-bodied animals, with shortish legs and a **brain** the size of a chimpanzee's. They probably lived largely on a diet of fruit, supplemented by whatever else they could obtain, including roots and tubers and small animals found on the ground. They were good climbers as well as upright walkers on the ground, and were very successful for a long time.

Long after they first appeared, about 2 1/2 million years ago, hominids like this began to make the first stone tools—as we saw in the last chapter. Only about half a million years later did a new kind of hominid show up. It was taller and with a body much more like our own, though with a brain only about half the size of ours. This new kind of hominid, belonging to our own genus, *Homo*, spread rapidly out of Africa and into Eurasia. But for a long time they still continued to use the old kind of stone tool.

Is that hominid going to be killed by the hyena?

Yes, and parts of him, maybe the head, taken away to the hyena's lair. In fact, hyenas were responsible for accumulating many of the hominid bones we now know as prized fossils!

carnivore teeth

Human skull fragment

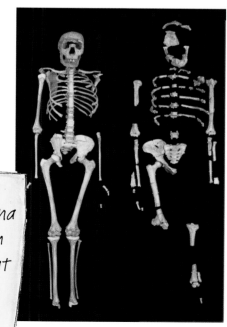

Lucy (right) was much smaller than the Turkana Boy, but showing them the same size brings out Lucy's short legs and wide pelvis.

Neanderthals! They were an ancient kind of human being that lived in Europe until about 30,000 years ago.

Moving around

Once **hominids** were out of Africa they spread widely, reaching Eastern Asia quite rapidly but arriving in Europe only about a million years ago. And in Africa they continued to evolve, too. By about 600 thousand years ago, a new species called *Homo heidelbergensis* had appeared there, and it also spread rapidly beyond its African birthplace. Although their **brains** were not quite as big as ours, it was members of this species that seem to have invented the first shelters and learned to control fire in hearths for cooking.

In Europe we have a very good **archaeological record**, and we know that independent evolution in this region eventually gave rise (about 200 thousand years ago) to a kind of hominid called

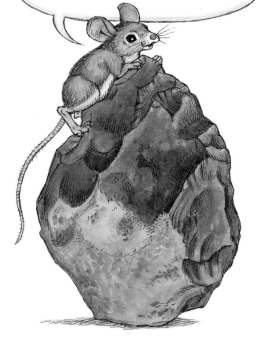

And within a few thousand years after the Cro-Magnons arrived, they disappeared.

European handaxe

34

Neanderthals were humans too, but Cro-Magnons almost certainly didn't mix with them.

They were a different species of human, you see. Look how different they are physically, not just in the shape of their heads but in their body shape.

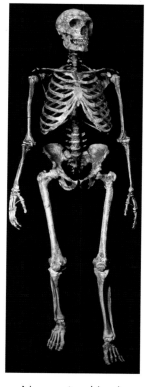

Check out the way the rib cage slopes out to meet the wide pelvis in Neanderthal, who would have moved differently from Homo sapiens as well as looking different.

Neanderthal

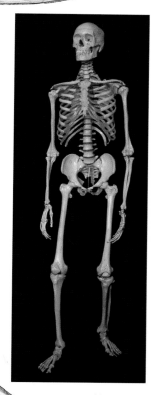

Homo sapiens

bone flute

the Neanderthals (*Homo neanderthalensis*) for a valley in Germany. The Neanderthals had **brains** as big as ours, made fancy **stone tools**, and buried their dead, but they did not make any carvings or other objects that might suggest they had **abstract thought**.

Eventually, the Neanderthals were replaced in Europe by new arrival, again with its roots in Africa. These immigrants were called the Cro-Magnons, and they belonged to our species, *Homo sapiens*. They painted on the walls of caves, made lovely carvings and engravings, and played musical instruments. Soon the Neanderthals were gone, and it seems that this pattern was repeated widely across the world. Before long, *Homo sapiens* was the only hominid species left.

So, you are wondering if the Cro-Magnons killed them off. We don't know for sure. It's likely they fought, but it may be that the Cro-Magnons were just better competitors and used the environment more efficiently. Probably a bit of both.

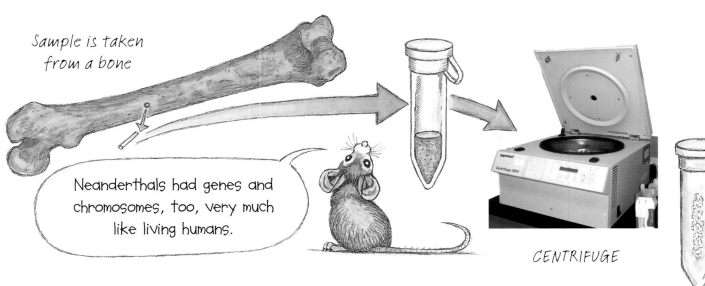

Sample is taken from a bone

Neanderthals had genes and chromosomes, too, very much like living humans.

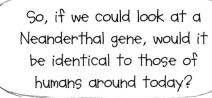

CENTRIFUGE

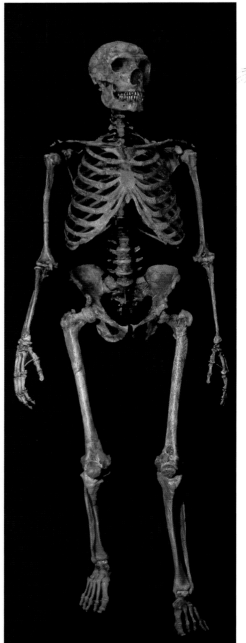

So, if we could look at a Neanderthal gene, would it be identical to those of humans around today?

Neanderthal DNA

By looking at DNA from **fossils**, we can understand some important ideas about how humans moved across the Earth. We can address questions of how and when humans emerged from Africa. One of the more interesting questions about ancient humans involves how they interacted when they came into contact with each other. Did the residents mate with the new arrivals? For instance, did the Neanderthals mate with the *Homo sapiens* (our species) that came to Europe a little later? All you need to do is get some Neanderthal DNA and see if there are traces of Neanderthal DNA in our species' DNA. Not so easy to get DNA from a fossil, right?

Well, actually, scientists have obtained information from **genes** from several Neanderthals. NO! It's not what you might be thinking; these guys are NOT alive today. By taking a drill bit and drilling into Neanderthal fossil bones, and then taking the powder produced by the drilling and isolating DNA from it,

It would be the same gene, but there would be a lot of changes in the DNA letters in the gene. In fact, there would be many more changes between a living human and a Neanderthal than between any two living humans.

Neanderthal DNA goes into a sequencer

DNA chains separated by electrophoresis

Too bad there are no Neanderthals still around. We could look at their DNA.

Oh, but scientists have isolated DNA from a Neanderthal's skeleton and analyzed it.

scientists were able to obtain enough Neanderthal DNA to get information on Neanderthal genes. This is a really difficult task, and scientists don't think they can get DNA from fossils much older than Neanderthals (30,000 to 40,000 years ago). The reason for this is that DNA in dead tissues and bones breaks down over time into tinier and tinier fragments until there is no information left.

What have the Neanderthal genes told us? They tell us that Neanderthals and **modern humans** (us) did not mate, and that modern humans replaced Neanderthals in Europe. Most likely a single wave of modern humans migrated to Europe about 40,000 years ago, and without mating with Neanderthals replaced them in most parts of Europe. How the *Homo sapiens* who first migrated did this is a mystery.

Get outa here! Really!

The sequence of Neanderthal DNA was first published in this journal.

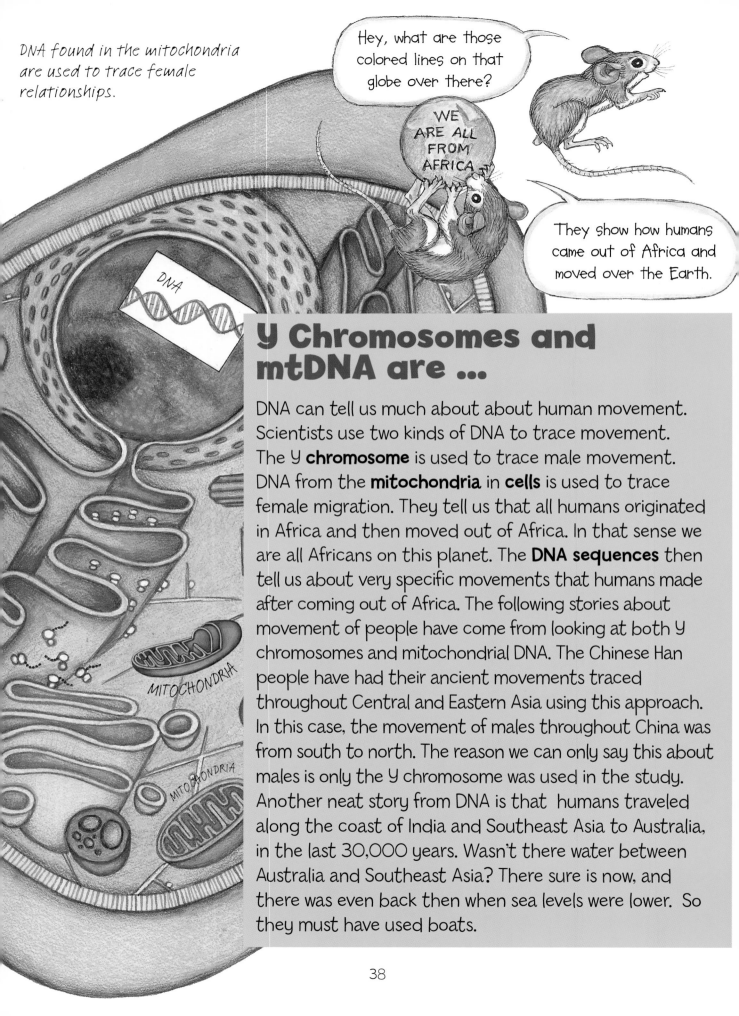

DNA found in the mitochondria are used to trace female relationships.

Hey, what are those colored lines on that globe over there?

WE ARE ALL FROM AFRICA

They show how humans came out of Africa and moved over the Earth.

DNA

MITOCHONDRIA

MITOCHONDRIA

Y Chromosomes and mtDNA are ...

DNA can tell us much about about human movement. Scientists use two kinds of DNA to trace movement. The Y **chromosome** is used to trace male movement. DNA from the **mitochondria** in **cells** is used to trace female migration. They tell us that all humans originated in Africa and then moved out of Africa. In that sense we are all Africans on this planet. The **DNA sequences** then tell us about very specific movements that humans made after coming out of Africa. The following stories about movement of people have come from looking at both Y chromosomes and mitochondrial DNA. The Chinese Han people have had their ancient movements traced throughout Central and Eastern Asia using this approach. In this case, the movement of males throughout China was from south to north. The reason we can only say this about males is only the Y chromosome was used in the study. Another neat story from DNA is that humans traveled along the coast of India and Southeast Asia to Australia, in the last 30,000 years. Wasn't there water between Australia and Southeast Asia? There sure is now, and there was even back then when sea levels were lower. So they must have used boats.

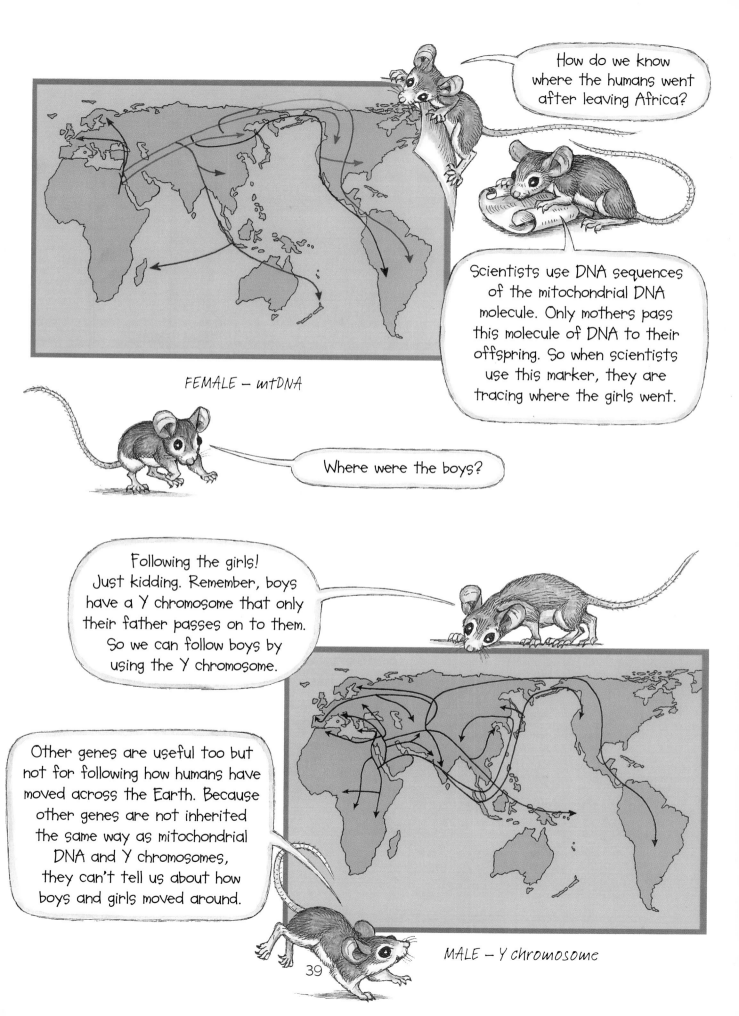

FEMALE — mtDNA

MALE — Y chromosome

Have you noticed all those fossil skulls? The more recent ones have bigger brains.

Chimpanzee

Australopithecus africanus

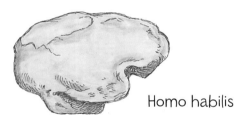

Homo habilis

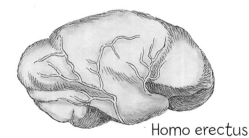

Homo erectus

Becoming Human

Human beings are different from their extinct and living relatives in many different ways. For example, only we walk on two legs, and that has made an enormous difference to what we look like. But to us the difference that really matters is that we are capable of thinking **abstract thoughts**, and of talking about them. Most importantly, it is our intelligence that makes us different.

We can see from the **archaeological record** that over time our **precursors** made more and more complex **stone tools**. And the **fossils** show us that over the past couple of million years, the **brains** of our extinct relatives increased remarkably in size. The obvious message here is that they were getting smarter, although not necessarily slowly and steadily. Intelligence seems to have increased in a series of steps.

Still, it doesn't seem that this increase in intelligence was just like climbing a ladder. As far as we can tell, the kind of intelligence we have is different from that of other animals, including our extinct relatives. None of them made paintings or sculptures, or played music. And most likely, smart though they were, they didn't tell each other stories, either.

Look. The earliest hominids had ape-size brains. That's about a third the size of ours, but brain size more than doubled by a million years ago. And look at us today.

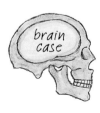

brain case

Homo sapiens

Hominids were getting smarter, but exactly what that means is difficult to say because most of the evidence consists of stone tools, which are only a tiny part of the whole lifestyle.

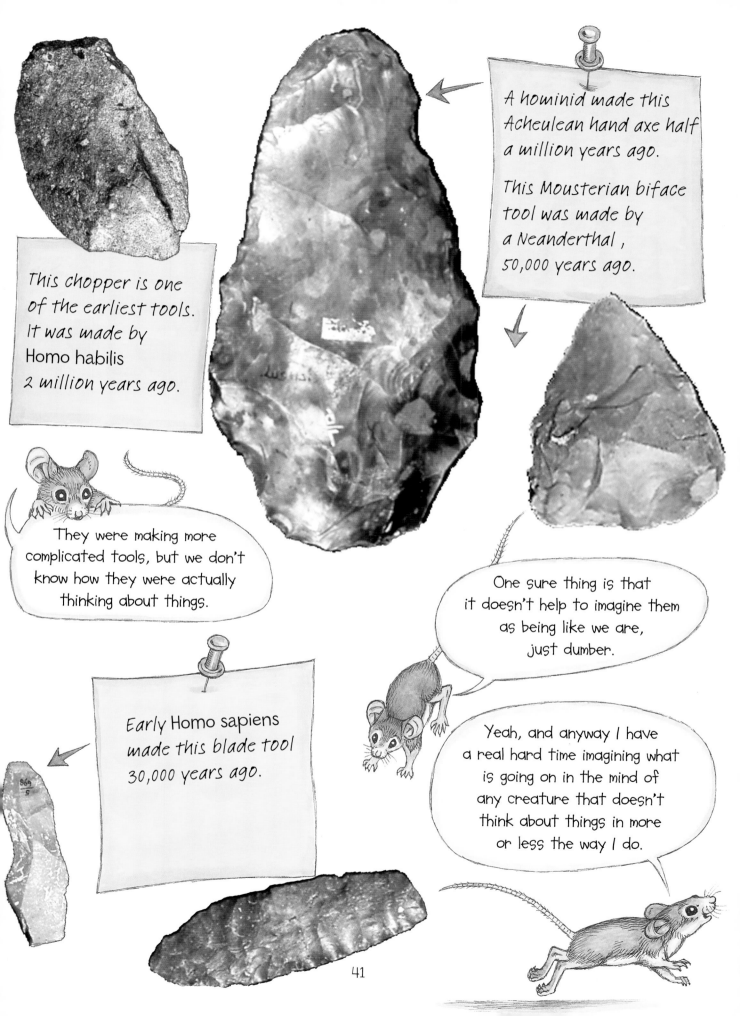

A hominid made this Acheulean hand axe half a million years ago.

This Mousterian biface tool was made by a Neanderthal, 50,000 years ago.

This chopper is one of the earliest tools. It was made by Homo habilis 2 million years ago.

They were making more complicated tools, but we don't know how they were actually thinking about things.

One sure thing is that it doesn't help to imagine them as being like we are, just dumber.

Early Homo sapiens made this blade tool 30,000 years ago.

Yeah, and anyway I have a real hard time imagining what is going on in the mind of any creature that doesn't think about things in more or less the way I do.

It says here that the early *Homo sapiens* in Israel seem to have behaved just like the Neanderthals who lived there.

Wooly Mammoth

How do you know if a hominid had language?

It's especially tricky to imagine how a really smart hominid that didn't have language actually experienced the world.

It's a really tough call, because before the invention of writing, all the evidence is indirect.

But there must be some giveaways.

Well, language is a symbolic activity, so if a hominid made symbolic objects of some kind, we can be pretty certain it had language.

Symbolic?

braids

perforated shell beads

spear-thrower with horse decoration

One thing that is clear from looking at the human **fossil** and **archaeological records** is that although both proceeded in a series of jumps, those jumps did not happen in synch. You can't use the appearance of a new **hominid** species to "explain" a new behavior. This actually makes sense, because any inventor of a new way of doing things must belong to a species that already exists!

We can be sure that our ancestors once did not have **abstract thought** or **language**. Yet today we have both. How did the change come about? Well, the earliest *Homo sapiens* seem to have behaved pretty much like earlier hominids that lacked these features, even though they were physically very different. And since we can fairly assume that the brain wiring that permits complex thought had been acquired along with all the other striking physical features of our species, it must have been a cultural rather than a **physical innovation** that sparked abstract thought in some population of the species *Homo sapiens*.

What might that innovation have been? One really good candidate is the invention of language. In order to use language, we create mental symbols in our heads and recombine them in new ways to come up with new ideas—which is what abstract thought is all about. Once language had been invented, it could then have spread among populations around the world that were already biologically prepared to receive it.

The Cro-Magnons made great art, and certainly had language. But beads and body ornaments are probably a pretty good pointer, and those are known in Africa as much as 75,000 years ago.

So, are humans still evolving? Are we mice still evolving?

Sure, evolution is just change with time and our genes are changing in our populations all the time.

Think about this. Humans have changed so much over 20,000 years; won't they evolve more quickly than any other species on the planet?

Future Evolution of humans

Think about the future. Where will your grandchildren be? Will they be smarter than you, bigger than you, more athletic than you? Will they live longer than you? Some scientists think that we will be able to alter the **genes** in our **genomes**. These altered genes will be able to make us healthier and live longer. But some scientists think that we might even be able to change our genes to make ourselves look better, be stronger, smarter, faster, and a whole slew of things that don't necessarily make us healthier. Should we let these gene changes happen? If we do, who will be able to use them? Who will make laws about them? These are all ethical questions, and all humans need to be aware of the changes that can be made and of how they might affect human evolution.

Some other changes that scientists foresee concern going into outer space. Think about this, and what it might do to how humans evolve. Humans will always explore things, so it is not unreasonable to think that

Homo sapiens   Australopithecus afarensis (Lucy)

44

Good question. Remember that a lot of the early human populations were tiny. In small populations things can change very rapidly.

Why's that, I wonder?

Say you flip a coin 100 times. You will probably flip on average 50 heads and 50 tails, right?

Sounds right.

HEADS   TAILS

Now flip 3 coins. There's a good chance that you will get 3 heads in a row. This means that with a small number of tries (like in a tiny human population) that chance strange events will happen.

humans will start to explore outer space in the near future. But just as our mice discuss above, the people who will go into space will do so in small groups, and hence the populations sent to explore might in their isolation experience more evolutionary change than the populations on Earth. How will space travel affect human evolution? What changes might happen in outer space that are relevant to human evolution? These are really neat questions, and we can't simply say that they won't happen.

We also know that humans can change the **environment** in drastic ways. Over the past 250 years, **industrialization** has changed the environment. Wars and disease can also have huge effects on the environment, and could have huge effects on the human future. As humans, we all need to be aware of our environment because it is vital to our survival. But as long as our population remains huge, it is unlikely that it will change much.

I get it. Because current human populations are really big and connected today, chance events are NOT going to happen.

Yes! And it is these chance events that really make changes in human evolution.

Glossary

Abstract Thought. Thinking that is based on creating and combining symbols (words) in the mind.

Adaptations. Alterations or adjustment in structure or habits, often hereditary, which improves a species' condition in relationship to its environment.

Anthropologist. A scientist who studies people, their cultures, and their prehistory.

Archaeological Record. The record of people's past behaviors as expressed by artifacts and other evidence of activity.

Archaeologist. A scientist who studies the material remains (artifacts, monuments, etc.) of past human life and activities.

Archaeology. The study of human cultures through the recovery, documentation, and analysis of material remains and environmental data, including architecture, artifacts, and human remains.

Autosomes. Chromosomes other than sex chromosomes.

Biological Anthropologists. Scientists who study people as biological rather than cultural beings.

Brain. In animals, the portion of the body that is the control center of the central nervous system.

Cell. A single unit or compartment, enclosed by a border, wall, or membrane.

Chromosome. A very long, continuous piece of DNA (a single DNA molecule), which contains many genes, regulatory elements, and other intervening nucleotide sequences.

Common Ancestry. The notion, proposed by Charles Darwin, that all organisms on Earth are descended from the same ancestral form.

Cone Cell. One of 6 million cone-shaped cells in the retina of the eye that help discriminate colors.

Cultural Anthropologist. A scientist who studies how people organize themselves socially, interact with each other, and understand the world around them.

Dating Methods. The various scientific ways of determining the age of rocks or fossils.

Descent with Modification. The basic pattern of evolution, whereby the whole diversity of life on Earth stems from changes passed down in different lineages of organisms.

Development of Organisms. The stages of a species' growth and change.

DNA. A nucleic acid (the chemical that makes up DNA) — usually in the form of a double helix — that contains the genetic instructions that specify the biological development of all cellular forms of life.

DNA Sequence. A succession of letters (GACT) representing the primary structure of a real or hypothetical DNA molecule or strand, with the capacity to carry information.

Double Helix. A spiral consisting of two strands in the surface of a cylinder that coil around its axis. The structural arrangement of DNA in space consists of paired polynucleotide (many DNA bases strung together) strands stabilized by cross-links between purine (another name for the bases G and A) and pyrimidine (another name for the bases C and T) bases.

Environment. The circumstances, objects, or conditions by which one is surrounded.

Evolution. A process of accumulating biological change over time.

Forest Canopy. The area above the forest floor where the tree crowns meet to form an interactive web of life.

Fossil. A remnant, impression, or trace of an organism of past geologic ages that has been preserved in the earth's crust

GACT. The four nucleotide subunits of a DNA strand are G(guanine), A(adenine), C(cytosine), and T(thymine). *See DNA Sequence*

Gene Expression. The process by which a gene's DNA sequence is converted into the structures and functions of a cell.

Genes. The units of heredity in living organisms encoded in its genetic material (usually DNA or RNA). They control the physical development and behavior of the organism.

Genome. The whole hereditary information of an organism that is encoded in its DNA.

Genus *Homo.* The group that includes modern humans and their close relatives.

Glossary. A list of terms with the definitions for those terms contained in a book.

Great Apes. The closest living relatives of humans: the chimpanzees, bonobos, gorillas, and orangutans.

Haemophilus influenza. The cause of septicemia and bacterial meningitis in young children.

Hereditary. Genetically transmitted or transmittable from parent to offspring.

Hominid. Any member of the zoological family Hominidae that contains humans and our close extinct relatives.

Homo heidelbergensis. "Heidelberg Man" is an extinct species of the genus *Homo* known from Africa, Europe, and probably Asia as well, in the period between about 600 and 200 thousand years ago.

Homo neanderthalensis. A species of the genus *Homo* that inhabited Europe and parts of western Asia between about 200 and 30 thousand years ago.

Homo sapiens. The species to which all living human beings belong. Latin for "knowing man."

Industrialization. The process of social and economic change from simpler economic patterns to large-scale industries.

Inherited Characteristics. Features of an organism that are passed along from parent to offspring.

Intelligence. The ability underlying the skilled use of reason to apply knowledge to manipulate one's environment or to think abstractly.

Language. A systematic means of communicating ideas or feelings by the use of a limited vocabulary that can be arranged according to the rules of syntax to express an unlimited range of meanings.

Lemurs. Our primate relatives that live on the island of Madagascar, and that are the closest living models of our own ancestors some 50 million years ago.

Lorises. Any of several nocturnal slow-moving tailless arboreal primates of southern and eastern Asia.

Mental Symbols. Ideas, images, or thoughts that are the basis for the creation of language.

Mitochondria. The cells' power sources that are distinct organelles with two membranes. Usually they are rod-shaped; however, they can be round.

Modern Humans (Us). Bipedal primates belonging to the mammalian species *Homo sapiens.*

Molecule. The smallest particle of a substance that retains all the properties of the substance and is composed of one or more atoms.

Monkeys. General term for two groups of "higher" primates (the larger group that also contains the greater and lesser apes and us): the South American monkeys, such as tamarins, howler monkeys, and so forth, and the African and Asian monkeys (such as baboons and langurs, respectively).

Natural Selection. The process whereby individuals better adjusted to their environments more successfully pass their genes along to their offspring.

Nucleus. The central portion of a complex cell that contains the DNA and chromosomes.

Organelle A discrete structure within a cell, such as a mitochondrion, that perform specialized functions.

Paleontologist. A scientist who studies past life as known from fossils.

Physical Innovation. A biological as opposed to a cultural originality in a species.

Precursor. A substance, cell, or cellular component from which another substance, cell, or cellular component is formed.

Recent Common Ancestor. The most recent relative shared by a group of species. *See Common Ancestry.*

Resemblance. The quality or state of resembling, particularly in appearance or superficial qualities.

Sex Chromosomes. The XX/XY sex-determination system is one of the most familiar sex-determination systems and is found in most mammals. In the XY sex-determination system, females have two of the same kind of sex chromosome (XX), while males have two distinct sex chromosomes (XY).

Similar. Having characteristics in common.

Stone Tool. Any implement made by modifying a piece of stone for a particular useful purpose.

Theory. A well-corroborated notion put forward to account for a particular set of observations of nature.

Tissues. A collection of cells usually of a particular kind, together with their intercellular substance, that form one of the structural materials of a plant or an animal.

X and Y chromosomes. *See Sex Chromosomes.*

Zoologist. A biologist concerned with the study of animals.

First published in 2007
by Bunker Hill Publishing Inc., 285 River Road,
Piermont, New Hampshire 03779, USA

10 9 8 7 6 5 4 3 2 1

Text copyright © Ian Tattersall and Rob DeSalle
Artwork copyright © Patricia J. Wynne
Illustrations copyright © American Museum of Natural History
Mural (pps 26-7) copyright ©Jay H. Matternes
Photos (pps 28 and 30) copyright © Willard Whitson

All rights reserved

Library of Congress Control Number: 2006931578

ISBN 1 59373 056 X

Designed by Louise Millar

Printed in China by Jade Productions Ltd

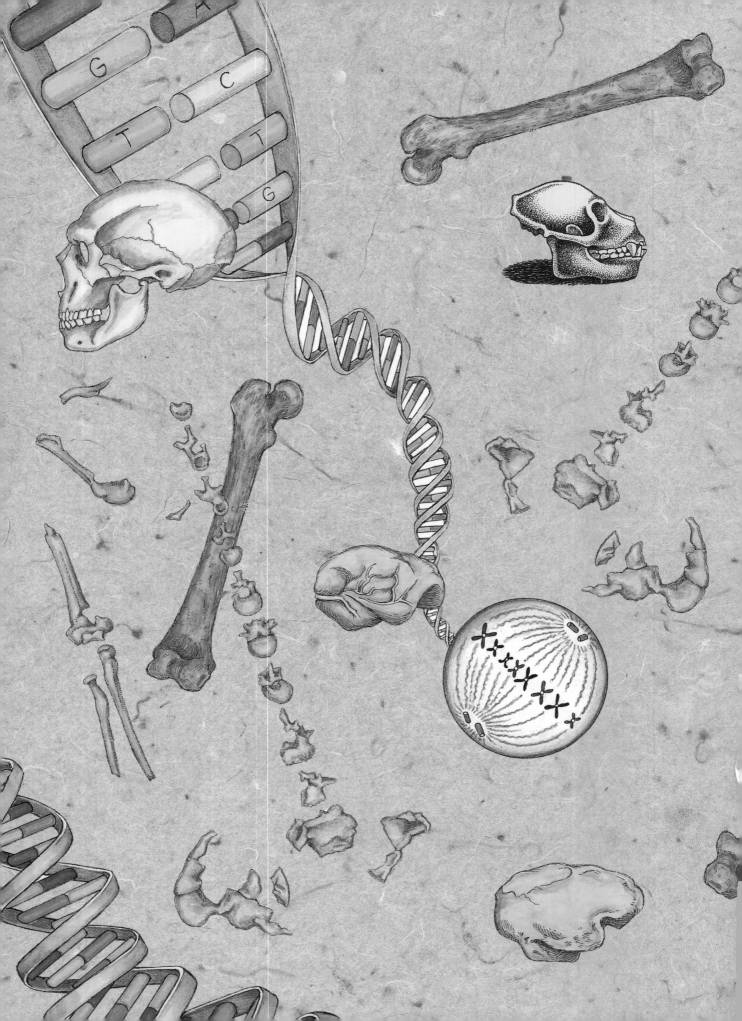